Alfie Potts™

THE SCHOOLBOY ENTREPRENEUR

Mark Hibbitts

Illustrated by Brendan Purchase

bookshaker

First Published in Great Britain 2011 by www.BookShaker.com

© Copyright Mark Hibbitts
Illustrations by Brendan Purchase

In Memory of Jim Rohn

September 25, 1930 – December 5, 2009

ALFIE GETS AN IDEA

Alfie Potts was an entrepreneur.

Unlike most twelve year old boys Alfie was learning how to get rich, and it had all started shortly before his twelfth birthday...

"Daaaad!" shouted Alfie. "Will you buy me a new Playstation? My best friend William just got one and they're awesome."

"Now Alfie," said Alfie's dad. "You know I don't believe in buying you things just for the sake of it. If I did that every time you wanted something you'd never value anything. I'll tell you what I'll do. If you can find a way to make half the money yourself, I'll give you the other half."

"But Dad, how will I do that?" asked Alfie.

"Making money isn't difficult Alfie," said his dad. "You just have to think of an idea"

"An idea?" said Alfie. "Is that all?"

"Yes Alfie. It's as simple as that," said his dad. "Successful people think of ideas all the time. Just take a look at some of the problems people face around here, and if you can think of a way to make that problem go away they'll gladly pay you for that. That's why I often say there's no such thing as a money problem, just an idea problem."

"Wicked!" laughed Alfie as he ran out of the door.

Alfie ran straight to William's house.

"William!" he shouted. "I've got work to do and I think I'll need your help."

"What do you mean, work?" said William, who was happily sitting on the couch watching telly. "It's the summer holidays."

"Listen," said Alfie. "My dad said he'd give me half the money for a new Playstation if I can make the other half, so I need to come up with an idea. Let's get thinking!"

"But Alfie, you're not even twelve yet, and you'll need nearly £150 to get that. How are you planning to make all that money?"

Alfie Potts sat on William's bed, scratching his chin thoughtfully. "I don't know yet William, but where there's a will there's a way. That's what Dad always tells me anyhow. I just need to think of an idea."

Ten minutes later Alfie jumped up from the bed. "I've got it" he exclaimed. "It's summer. What does everyone want in the summer?"

"I don't know Alfie, ice cream?" said William, hopefully.

"No." said Alfie. "Well yes, but that's not what I meant. There's nearly 200 houses on Fortune Street alone, and they all need their grass cutting. If I charge a fiver a time I'll soon make enough money. Turn your computer on William. Let's make some flyers."

The boys spent the next hour designing and printing a flyer that Alfie could post through all the letterboxes on his street. It looked like this...

ALFIE'S GRASS CUTTING SERVICES

WHY DON'T YOU RELAX
AND ENJOY THIS LOVELY SUNSHINE!

IF YOU HAVE A LAWNMOWER
I'LL CUT YOUR GRASS FOR YOU

ONLY £5 PER LAWN

Alfie Potts
3 Fortune Street
Call me on 555 6749 or 07755 665443

"Right," said Alfie. "William, will you give me a hand posting these, please?"

"Of course," said William and they headed out of the door

That evening Alfie got a call on his mobile phone.

"Hello? Is that Alfie? This is Mr Smith at number 11. Could you cut my grass tomorrow please? You can? 10 o'clock? That's great. Just knock on the back door and Mrs Smith will show you where the mower is."

"Yes!" shouted Alfie, punching the air. "I'm in business!"

3 more calls came that evening, so when Alfie woke up the next morning and the sun was shining he knew he had a busy day ahead...

...Phew! It was hot!

As Alfie mowed his last lawn of the day he was sweating, but he didn't mind.

His hand drifted to his pocket. He could feel the £15 he had earned so far, and the knowledge there was another five pound note coming shortly spurred him on to get the job finished.

Also, he had received 4 more calls on his mobile, and his mum had just rung to say he's had another 6 bookings on the home phone.

"I'll have the money for my Playstation in no time if I carry on like this" he thought to himself.

But then something stopped him dead in his tracks...

"Wait a minute!" said Alfie out loud. "How on earth am I going to mow 10 lawns tomorrow? This is only my fourth today and I'm tired already!"

He thought for a moment.

"I think I'd better ask Dad when I get home. He ALWAYS knows what to do."

A LESSON FROM DAD

"How did your day go son?" asked his dad, later that evening.

"It was great," said Alfie. "I made twenty quid cutting the neighbours grass," and he showed the 4 crisp fivers to his dad.

"Well done son! Your first real wages!" exclaimed Dad. "How do you feel about that?"

"Pretty good actually," said Alfie. "Making money doesn't seem that difficult when you put your mind to it, but I do need your advice on something Dad. I'm a bit worried about tomorrow."

"Why's that son?"

"Well," began Alfie, "by 2 o'clock this afternoon I had 10 more people wanting me to cut their grass tomorrow, and by this evening I'd had another 6 calls. It seems that no one wants to cut their grass in this hot weather. I guess that's good news for me dad, but I can't possibly do all that tomorrow on my own. Do you have any ideas?"

"I'm really proud of you Alfie," said his Dad. "You had a great idea, and if you're able to solve problems for people like this you'll have a very successful life. Now stop worrying, when you're in business for yourself it's better to have too much work than too little. All you need to do is get some leverage."

"Leverage?" asked Alfie. "What's leverage, and where do I get it?"

His dad laughed. "Leverage, Alfie, is how you get rich. There's not a wealthy person in the world who doesn't have leverage working for them in some way, shape or form!"

"That sounds great Dad!" exclaimed Alfie, "but what is it and how do I get it?"

"Come and sit over here with me Alfie," said his Dad, "and I'll tell you. Pay close attention, because they don't teach you this stuff in school!"

"Today, Alfie, like most people, what you did was traded your time for money. Each lawn you cut took an hour or so, and for each one you earned yourself £5. You did very well son, but if you carry on trading time for money there will always be a limit to what you can earn. Even if someone makes lots of money per hour, there are only so many hours in the day they can work. Do you understand what I mean?"

"Yes dad. I think so. Even if someone earns £100 an hour there's only 24 hours in a day, and they won't be able to work all of those!"

"That's very good son," said Alfie's dad, smiling. "You're a quick learner, but the sad thing is most people never learn about this. They spend their whole lives working in that time for money trap, and they become like hamsters in a wheel, thinking if they can only get another little raise everything will be ok."

"Really?" said Alfie. "That's terrible!"

"Yes it is son. But once you learn about leverage you won't have to do that anymore."

"Then you'd better tell me more," said Alfie eagerly.

"One day Alfie, a very wise man told me that PROFITS ARE BETTER THAN WAGES. He said WAGES WILL MAKE YOU A LIVING, WHILE PROFITS MAKE YOU A FORTUNE. The man's name was Jim Rohn son, and when he told you something, you listened."

"So let's take a look at what he meant. Today you earned yourself some wages which is good, but tomorrow, if you can get some leverage in your grass cutting business, you can earn yourself some profits. And that, Alfie, would be really good."

"I'm not sure I understand what you mean," said Alfie.

"I haven't finished yet son. Do you know who Richard Branson is?"

"Yes Dad. He's that billionaire with the long hair and the smile isn't he?"

"Yes Alfie. That's the one. Well Richard Branson and others like him understand leverage. He has businesses all over the world. How many people do you think he has working for him?"

"I don't know dad," said Alfie. "Thousands?"

"You may be right son. And all those people are working in his businesses because it means much more work gets done than if Richard was working all by himself. They give him leverage. Are you starting to understand what I'm saying?"

"Yes dad. At least I think so." Said Alfie, frowning.

Good. Well Richard pays them all different wages depending on the job they do, but they actually make him more money than he pays them. In other words he makes a profit on each of them, which is why he can spend a lot of time in the sun on his private island.

"That's just lazy!" frowned Alfie.

Alfie's dad chuckled. "Not at all Alfie" he said. "It's just good business. Richard Branson is an entrepreneur and it's entrepreneurs like him that make the world go round. They work very hard and they have great vision. They look at all the problems people face, and then come up with the answers to those problems, just like you did today Alfie. Entrepreneurs are the ones who provide products and services for people all around the world and they give jobs to millions of people. They are the ones who take risks and who are willing to do what other people won't do. Because they do that, they end up being able to do what other people can't do, like owning an island. Of course it's true that entrepreneurs can make lots of money, but that's only because of the value they bring to the world. In reality son, they deserve every penny they get.

"Dad?" said Alfie.

"Yes son?"

"I want to be an entrepreneur."

Alfie's Dad put his arm round Alfie and gave him a squeeze.

"You already are son," he said proudly, "you already are."

ALFIE GETS SOME LEVERAGE

Alfie thought for a while.

"Dad," he said suddenly, "I'm only cutting people's grass, not solving the world's problems like Richard Branson does. How does someone like me get leverage?"

"Well son, here's a thought for you. How many of your school friends do you think would like to make a little money this summer?"

"Most of them I reckon," said Alfie.

"Well I reckon so too," said his dad, "and you earned £20 yesterday didn't you? That's quite a lot for an eleven year old don't you think?"

"Yes dad," said Alfie proudly. "I'd have done it for half that much."

"Exactly!" exclaimed his dad "And so will your friends. You have 16 lawns to cut tomorrow. How much money will that give you?"

"Um ... sixteen times a fiver ... that's £80," said Alfie.

"That's right son. And do you think your friends would work for £12 a day?"

"I'm sure they would!" answered Alfie excitedly, starting to get the picture.

"Ok. So what would happen if you paid three of your friends £3 a lawn, and got them to cut 4 lawns each tomorrow too?"

Alfie thought for a moment, "They'd make £12 each?"

"Yes son, and 3 times £12 is £36. That means you'd pay them £36 in wages. Take that off the £80 you'll take in and that leaves you with what?"

"£44," replied Alfie quickly.

"That's right son, and that's your profit. In other words, yesterday you worked very hard and made £20. Tomorrow you could do the same amount of work yourself, and make £44 instead of £20. Which sounds better to you?"

"The £44 of course!" said Alfie.

"I thought it would," said Alfie's dad. "And that, Alfie, is leverage!"

"Thanks dad, that's awesome!" said Alfie, getting up quickly and running towards the door. "I'd better make some phone calls. I'm recruiting!"

ALFIE GETS HIS MONEY

By 9.30 the next morning there were three bikes leaned up against the garden fence, and William, Sahid, and T.J were all in Alfies kitchen reporting for duty.

Getting his friends involved had been a doddle. The promise of £12 for a few hours work in the holidays was too good to be missed. In fact, he'd only had to make 4 calls to get the 3 that he needed, and his friend Kyle, the recipient of the other call, was disappointed not to be able to help out.

"I'm sorry Alfie," he said. "I'm gutted, but I have to go to my gran's with mum and dad tomorrow. I'd love to earn twelve quid. Really I would. If I can help you any other time please call me."

"No worries. I will," said Alfie with a grin.

Alfie stood in the kitchen and spoke to his friends.

"Right," he said, "my dad says that if we provide a good service our customers will tell other people, and we'll have enough work to last us all through the holidays."

"Yay!" cried T.J. "That's good! We're all going to be rich!"

"Maybe we are," replied Alfie, "but dad also says that if we provide a bad service people will talk even more, and we'll be out of business before we get going."

"That's not so good," said Sahid. "What's the plan then Alfie?"

"Well, we have to be on time, we have to be polite and courteous, and we have to do a good job. That means finishing everything properly, clearing up afterwards, and not leaving a mess. You can all do that can't you?" asked Alfie.

"Of course we can!" the boys replied, eagerly.

"Good. Oh, there's one more thing," said Alfie. "Dad says we should always ask for referrals."

"What's a referral?" asked T.J.

"It's when someone is happy with your work and they let other people know about you, or give you the name of a friend that would also like your services," replied Alfie. "Dad says you get more business that way. To make it easy for you I've printed off these leaflets. Just give one to everyone when you've finished"

Alfie passed around the leaflets.

ALFIE'S GRASS CUTTING SERVICES
WE HOPE YOU'RE HAPPY WITH OUR SERVICE

IF YOU'RE NOT, PLEASE TELL US
IF YOU ARE, PLEASE TELL A FRIEND (OR 2)

Alfie Potts
3 Fortune Street
Call me on 555 6749 or 07755 665443

"Right, let's get to work!" he said.

Business was very good that summer!

Word of Alfie's venture soon spread, and it wasn't long until people 3 and 4 streets away were calling to get their lawns cut. Thankfully that wasn't a problem for Alfie, because there seemed to be an endless supply of boys and girls wanting to work for him.

In fact there were too many, and that was bothering Alfie.

One day, after telling yet another 12 year old boy there was nothing for him to do that day, he had another idea.

"Dad," he asked, "could you take me down to Halfords please?"

"Of course son," said his dad. "What are you scheming this time?"

Alfie grinned. "Drive me down there dad, and I'll show you," he replied.

When they got there, Alfie got a trolley and started filling it with buckets, sponges, cloths, shammy leathers, and wax polish.

"All my friends from school keep asking me for work dad," he said as he went up and down the aisles filling his trolley. "I don't always have enough lawns for them to cut and that means I'm losing money. I think if I invest some of my profits in a car washing business, I can probably double my income."

And that's just what he did!

By the end of the summer holidays Alfie had banked more than £2000 from his grass cutting and car washing businesses, and all his friends had made money too.

Everyone was happy!

"Alfie?" asked his dad one day, on the way to the bank. "You made enough money for your PlayStation weeks ago. Isn't it about time we went and bought it?"

"You know what dad?" said Alfie. "If I'd had it, I'd have wasted the whole summer holiday playing with it. Because I DIDN'T have it, look at what I've done instead! PlayStations are ok, but solving problems and making money is MUCH more fun!"

Alfie Potts was an entrepreneur!

Alfie Potts™

THE SCHOOLBOY ENTREPRENEUR

Now It's Your Turn...

If you're planning to be the next young entrepreneur then head over to this TOP SECRET page where Alfie's friends have got together to provide you with some cool free gifts including mind-bending hypnosis audios, workbooks and more...

www.alfiepotts.com/bonus-1

Printed in Great Britain
by Amazon